COLONIAL

TOWNS

Verna Fisher

Nomad Press
A division of Nomad Communications
10 9 8 7 6 5 4 3 2 1
Copyright © 2011 by Nomad Press.
All rights reserved.

This book was manufactured by
Regal Printing Limited in China
June 2011, Job #1105033
ISBN: 978-1-936313-61-7

Illustrations by Andrew Christensen
Educational Consultant, Marla Conn

Questions regarding the ordering of this book should be addressed to
Independent Publishers Group
814 N. Franklin St.
Chicago, IL 60610
www.ipgbook.com

Nomad Press
2456 Christian St.
White River Junction, VT 05001
www.nomadpress.net

Contents

MAP & TIMELINE ~ iii

CHAPTER 1 ~ PAGE 1
Busy Towns

CHAPTER 2 ~ PAGE 7
Getting Around

CHAPTER 3 ~ PAGE 13
The Arts

CHAPTER 4 ~ PAGE 17
Spread the Word

CHAPTER 5 ~ PAGE 21
Native American Villages

Glossary ~ Further Investigations ~ Index

Colonial America

3.

4.

12.

2.

6. **7.**

11.

1.

5. **8.**

★ ★ ★ ★ ★

Middle Colonies

New York,
New Jersey,
Pennsylvania,
Delaware, and
Maryland.

★ ★ ★ ★ ★

9.

10.

13.

★ ★ ★ ★ ★

Southern Colonies

Virginia, North Carolina,
South Carolina,
and Georgia.

★ ★ ★ ★ ★

N
W ⊕ E
S

New England

Massachusetts,
New Hampshire, Connecticut,
and Rhode Island.

In the 1600s, people began leaving Europe to settle in America. Some were explorers searching for gold, while others came looking for freedom.

Jamestown in Virginia and Plymouth in Massachusetts were two of the earliest settlements where these people came to start a new life.

1607

1. Virginia
2. Massachusetts
3. New York
4. New Hampshire
5. Maryland
6. Connecticut
7. Rhode Island
8. Delaware
9. North Carolina
10. South Carolina
11. New Jersey
12. Pennsylvania
13. Georgia

1733

Busy Towns

In **Colonial America**, many families lived in towns. These towns had shops, churches, **taverns**, schools, and houses. Colonial towns also had a central park. Here families could relax, talk with friends, and play. In most towns, the church was located by the park.

Colonial America: the name given to this country when talking about the years 1607–1776.

tavern: a place to get food or spend the night.

Boston Common was built in 1634. It is the oldest public park in the United States.

coast: the edge of the land near the sea.

seaport: where ships unload and load goods for sale.

colonist: a person who came to settle America.

New World: what settlers from Europe called America because it was new to them.

Words to Know

Towns along the **coast** and on large rivers grew quickly. These were busy **seaports** where ships from Europe stopped. The ships brought the **colonists** sugar, tea, cloth, books, and other goods not available in the **New World**.

The largest seaports were Boston in Massachusetts, New York City in New York, and Philadelphia in Pennsylvania. Other important seaports were smaller. These included Newport in Rhode Island, Baltimore in Maryland, and Charleston in South Carolina.

Did You Know?

The name of Philadelphia comes from the Greek word for "brotherly love." Philadelphia was the United States capital from 1790 to 1800.

Words to Know

In New England, many families could not earn money by farming. The soil was poor and the weather was cold. They could only grow enough **crops** to feed their families. In Boston, men worked building ships or fishing. They sold **goods** like furs to ships going to Europe.

In colonial times, Philadelphia grew to a **population** of 40,000. It was the largest city in the colonies.

Today, New York City has more than 8 million people. It is larger than any other city in the United States.

In the Middle and Southern Colonies, the soil and warm weather was better for growing crops. These colonists sent farm products on the ships to Europe. They also sold animal skins and **timber**.

Getting Around

In Colonial America, **transportation** was hard. Most travel was by men who needed to get to other colonies to sell their goods. Many colonists never left the place where they were born.

Words to Know

Roads were rough and full
of ruts. Often, colonists had
to walk slowly while pulling
a horse. The roads were
muddy when it rained.
They were dusty when
it was dry. Getting to
another colony could
take days, or even weeks.

Travel by water was
common. Most of the
larger towns were by the water.
Sailing ships carried passengers and
goods by sea between seaports.
Smaller boats and canoes travelled
waterways throughout the colonies.

Words to Know

In 1730, German settlers in Pennsylvania invented the Conestoga wagon. Up to six horses pulled these covered wagons. They carried people and hauled heavy loads of flour, wheat, and other goods. The wagon's wide wheels helped it get through mud without getting stuck.

By the end of the colonial period, **stagecoaches** carried passengers between towns and cities. Early stagecoaches were not comfortable. Colonists bumped along on benches without backs to lean against.

Then and Now

In colonial times, it took more than three days to go from Boston to New York City by stagecoach.

Today, we can drive between Boston and New York City in four hours.

Around town, colonists used simple carts with two wheels. The carts carried items like **produce** and firewood to shops in town. A colonist building a house could haul bricks in a cart.

A **wheelwright** fixed wheels, like mechanics repair cars and trucks today.

Because almost every family needed a cart, wheelwrights had an important job. Wheelwrights built wooden wheels that handled rough roads and bumpy fields.

The Arts

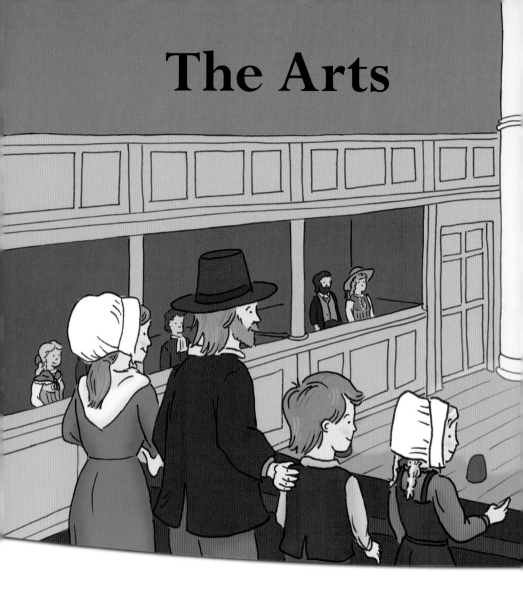

In the larger towns, people went to the theater to enjoy acting, singing, and dancing. Early theaters in America were built in the Southern Colonies in Williamsburg, Virginia, and in Charleston, South Carolina.

In the Puritan towns of New England, it was forbidden by law to put on a play.

The wealthiest colonists sat in fancy raised boxes on the sides of the stage. Other colonists sat on wooden benches in the center of the theater. Students, sailors, and slaves sat in the gallery above.

traveling artist: a painter, actor, singer, or dancer who travels from place to place.

portrait: a painting of one or more people.

canvas: cloth used for paintings.

Words to Know

Did You Know?

There were no cameras in Colonial America. A portrait was the only way to have a picture of yourself.

Traveling artists came from Europe to paint **portraits** for wealthy families. Soon, colonists learned to paint portraits. There were no art schools in Colonial America, so most painters taught themselves this new skill.

It took a long time to paint a portrait. To be faster and cheaper, artists painted bodies and backgrounds on **canvases** during the winter. In summer, they traveled around to different towns and quickly painted the heads to finish the portrait.

Spread the Word

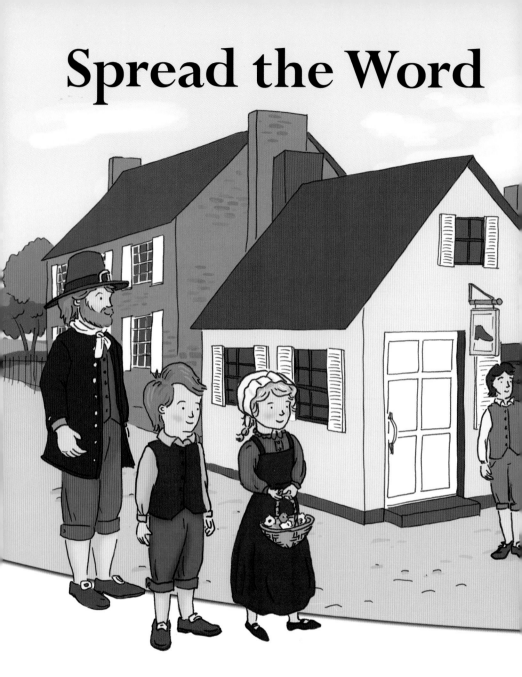

Most colonial towns had a **town crier** to spread public news. The town crier got people's attention by ringing a bell and shouting "hear ye, hear ye."

Words to Know

The town crier usually wore robes with bright colors, as well as white **breeches** and a three-cornered hat.

He would walk through the streets shouting the news. People wanted to know who was getting married or the details of an upcoming parade.

printing press: a machine for printing ink onto paper.

Benjamin Franklin: a famous colonial inventor. He was known for discovering the lightning rod.

publish: to print newspapers or books.

Words to Know

Before long, newspapers replaced town criers. The first **printing press** was brought from England to Cambridge, Massachusetts, in 1639.

Benjamin Franklin's *Pennsylvania Gazette* became a popular newspaper throughout the colonies. He also **published** *Poor Richard's Almanac* each year, starting in 1732. The almanac was filled with weather forecasts, puzzles, and poems the colonists enjoyed.

In colonial times, the town crier was an important job because it meant being able to read and write.

Native American Villages

Native American **tribes** lived all over America. They were there for thousands of years before the colonists arrived. As colonial towns spread, many tribes were forced to move their villages. They needed space to hunt, plant crops, and fish.

Words to Know

The Wampanoag tribe in New England lived in small, round houses called **wigwams**. They built their wigwams around a central square. The Iroquois in New York and the Powhatans in Virginia lived in **longhouses**. As many as ten families shared each longhouse.

nomadic: when a group moves around to find food.

tipi: a house like a tent built from poles, covered with bark or animal skin.

Words to Know

Some tribes, such as the Cherokee of the South, were **nomadic**. They had summer and winter villages. These tribes lived in **tipis** that were easy to build and move.

In any village, children helped gather food. They looked for wild nuts, fruits, and vegetables. They found eggs laid by birds and turtles. Native American kids played with balls, marbles, and dolls. They hid in houses and trees for hide-and-seek, just like kids do today.

Did You Know?

Many American states and cities are named after Native American words or names. Chicago is Algonquian for "garlic field."

Glossary

Benjamin Franklin: a famous colonial inventor. He was known for discovering the lightning rod.

breeches: tight pants that go to the knees.

canvas: cloth used for paintings.

coast: the edge of the land near the sea.

Colonial America: the name given to this country when talking about the years 1607–1776.

colonist: a person who came to settle America.

crop: a plant grown for food.

goods: things to use or sell.

longhouse: a house shaped like a rectangle with round corners, covered with bark.

New World: what settlers from Europe called America because it was new to them.

nomadic: when a group moves around to find food.

population: the number of people living in an area.

portrait: a painting of one or more people.

printing press: a machine for printing ink onto paper.

produce: farm products, especially fruits and vegetables.

publish: to print newspapers or books.

seaport: where ships unload and load goods for sale.

stagecoach: a heavy, closed vehicle on wheels, pulled by horses.

tavern: a place to get food or spend the night.

timber: wood used to build homes, ships, and other things.

tipi: a house like a tent built from poles, covered with bark or animal skin.

town crier: a person who shouted public news in the streets.

transportation: moving people or goods from one place to another.

traveling artist: a painter, actor, singer, or dancer who travels from place to place.

tribe: a large group of people with common ancestors and customs. Today, Native Americans use the word nation instead.

waterway: a stream or river that is wide and deep enough for a boat to travel on.

wheelwright: someone that builds and repairs wheels.

wigwam: a dome-shaped house made with poles, covered by bark or grass.

Further Investigations

Books

Bordessa, Kris. *Great Colonial America Projects You Can Build Yourself.* White River Junction, VT: Nomad Press, 2006.

Fisher, Verna. *Explore Colonial America! 25 Great Projects, Activities, Experiments.* White River Junction, VT: Nomad Press, 2009.

Museums and Websites

Colonial Williamsburg
www.history.org
Williamsburg, Virginia

National Museum of the American Indian
www.nmai.si.edu
Washington, D.C. and
New York, New York

Plimoth Plantation
www.plimoth.org
Plymouth, Massachusetts

America's Library
www.americaslibrary.gov

Jamestown Settlement
www.historyisfun.org

Native American History
www.bigorrin.org

Native Languages of the Americas
www.native-languages.org

Social Studies for Kids
www.socialstudiesforkids.com

The Mayflower
www.mayflowerhistory.com

Virtual Jamestown
www.virtualjamestown.org

Index

A
the arts, 13–16

B
Baltimore, Maryland, 3
Boston, Massachusetts,
  2, 3, 5, 10

C
carts, 11–12
central parks, 1–2
Charleston, South Carolina,
  3, 13
churches, 1
Conestoga wagons, 9

F
farms/farming, 5–6
food, 3, 5, 9, 23
Franklin, Benjamin, 19

G
goods, trade/sale
  of, 3, 5, 7, 8, 9

H
homes, 1, 22–23

M
map of colonies, iii
Middle Colonies,
  iii, 3, 4, 6, 10

N
Native American
  villages, 21–24
New England Colonies,
  iv, 2, 3, 5, 10, 13, 22
Newport, Rhode Island, 3
news delivery, 17–20
newspapers, 19
New York City, New
  York, 3, 6, 10

P
painting/portraits, 16
parks, 1–2
Philadelphia,
  Pennsylvania, 3, 4, 6
port cities, 3–6, 8, 13

R
roads, 8, 12

S
settlement of colonies,
  iii–iv
ships, 3, 5, 6, 8
Southern Colonies, iii, 3,
  6, 13
stagecoaches, 9

T
theaters, 13–14
town criers, 17–19, 20
transportation, 7–12
traveling artists, 16

W
wagons, 9
wheelwrights, 12
Williamsburg, Virginia, 13